Slave Mentality

"Break Free to Financial and Spiritual Freedom"

A.J.

May God continue to bless you abundantly!

John 10:10

Darlene J. Cotton

Darlene J. Cotton

Slave Mentality
"Break Free to Financial and Spiritual Freedom"

Published by Mentality Shift LLC, Atlanta, GA.
Copyright © 2018 by Darlene J. Cotton
ISBN-13:978-1-7327534-0-2

Disclaimer and Limit of Liability

Although anyone may find the teachings, practices, disciplines, techniques, examples, and anecdotes in this book useful, the book is sold with the understanding that neither the author nor publisher are engaged in presenting any specific financial, tax, career, legal, psychological, emotional or health advice. Nor is anything in this book an analysis, recommendation, solution, diagnosis, prognosis, or cure for any specific career, financial, psychological, emotional or relational circumstances. This book does not take those individual needs and circumstances into account. Any person experiencing financial or career concerns, or any anxiety, depression, stress, health or relationship issues, should consult with a financial or tax advisor, career counselor, medical doctor, licensed psychologist, licensed therapist, or other appropriate qualified professional before commencing any new financial plan or transaction, career strategy, change in personal relationships or following any of the teachings, methods and suggestions described in this book. This book is not to substitute for the reader enlisting qualified professionals to assist with the reader's specific circumstances, issues and problems.

The author and publisher specifically disclaim any liability, loss, or risk that is incurred as an outcome, directly or indirectly, through the use and application of any and all content contained in this book.

Edited by Cindy Davis, Mark Allen Kelly and Judi Fennell

Praise for Slave Mentality

"What I love about Darlene's book Slave Mentality is that her strategies for leaving debt and the poverty mindset behind are simple, practical and easy to understand. The exercises are designed to help you experience breakthrough in every chapter. The most powerful part in my opinion is forgiveness. If you don't have all that you desire, there is likely some unforgiveness in the way because God is not holding anything back from you. I'm grateful for Darlene's courage to take a stand for ending the poverty mindset and equipping people with all they need to shift into the abundance that is waiting for them when they take hold of the principles in this book. If you are ready to move from poverty to profit in every area of your life, this book is the road map you need to make the leap."

-Darnyelle Jervey Harmon, MBA CEO of Incredible One Enterprises, LLC.

CONTENTS

ACKNOWLEDGMENTS

This book would not have been written without the prompting of the Holy Spirit. Through the entire process of writing, I was challenged spiritually, mentally, physically, and financially. As a result of all the challenges my family and I went through in the process of writing this book, I have a more intense intimate trust in God. I now understand that He was taking me "through" those challenges so that I could be used to reach others.

To my husband Thomas, I thank you so much for your selfless sacrifices made during this entire process. I love you. You showed me patience, love and support even during the times you wondered why the book wasn't finished.

Thank you to my children, Joshua and Tyson, who at times had to go to bed earlier than normal so Mommy could work on finishing the book. My prayer is that this inspires you both to believe for yourselves that *"With God All Things Are Possible!"*

To my mom, Sheena, one of my biggest supporters, who has always encouraged and believed in me. I love you.

To my dad, Dieter, thank you for your love and being a good example of what it looks like to be financially responsible for your family and household. I love you.

To my good friend and bestselling author, Sharon C. Cooper. Thank you for sharing your knowledge, resources, encouragement, and supporting me through this process.

To my family and friends that prayed for me. Thank you so much. I love you.

The personal transformation I experienced while writing this book has been amazing, and I am so GRATEFUL! I pray the same for you as you read my book, may the Lord transform your life spiritually and financially beyond what you ever imagined as you experience the abundance Jesus sacrificed to give you!

FOREWORD

IN GOD WE TRUST is gently placed on the back of the United States dollar bill, however, the front prominently boasts the words *Federal Reserve Note.* If you take a closer look at the fine print, you will find the words *This note is legal tender for all debts, public and private.* I find it no coincidence that we put more emphasis and trust in this piece of paper than we do in God. Money serves as an agreement of trust in exchange for something we want. Culture has caused us to put our faith and trust in the almighty dollar. In all honesty, we really only want the freedom of choice that money provides us. Without that freedom of choice, the paper dollar is useless.

Darlene Cotton literally flips the order of this trust agreement in her book "$lave Mentality: Break Free to Financial and Spiritual Freedom" by eloquently weaving together our spiritual, emotional and financial selves. It was through her personal financial disruption during the foreclosure crisis that she recognized divine intervention was needed to relieve her of the insurmountable debt she was enslaved by. In addition to seeking spiritual wisdom and guidance, Darlene and her family sought the advice of a financial expert and they began to shift their money mindset from spending and borrowing to building personal wealth for themselves and the greater community. Darlene openly shares her story and experience with hope that others will learn from her financial pitfalls and begin to experience the financial and spiritual freedom God desires for all.

As a financial advisor, personal finance expert and workshop facilitator, I have been afforded the opportunity to use, view and opine on many financial education and personal finance curriculums, toolkits and applications over the past 21 years. Therefore, there are not many new concepts or strategies I have not been privy to. However, from start to finish, this book captured my attention with its innovation. Darlene's presentation of the discovery process and concepts are relatable and easy to follow. She skillfully walks the reader through a series of common financial challenges and provides exercises that force the reader to address their emotions as it relates money. Each exercise provides practical steps to overcome these challenges and references scripture that illuminates how the reader should view and address them in the spiritual realm. If you are looking to improve your inner financial self, this self-led financial and spiritual freedom journey is sure to provide you with a new mindset as it relates to your finances.

"Wealth is the ability to fully experience life."
~*Henry David Thoreau*

"We are buried beneath the weight of information, which is being confused with knowledge, quantity is being confused with abundance and wealth with happiness."
~ *Tom Watts*

Break Free to Financial and Spiritual Freedom

Sibyl S. Slade, CRPC
Former Senior Regional Community Development Manager, Federal Reserve Bank of Atlanta
Former Member of the Financial Literacy and Education Committee, U.S. Treasury
Atlanta, Georgia

Synopsis

Are you overwhelmed by never ending financial obligations or lack of sufficient income that has affected your health, put a strain on your relationships and robbed you of time to pursue what you truly crave in life?

Slave Mentality shows you how to break free from financial and spiritual bondage by providing empowerment through real life examples, biblical scriptures, prayer and study questions.

In this book you will learn:

➢ Easy to follow steps to shift your mindset from operating out of lack to living an abundant life.
➢ Ways to regain control of your finances and eliminate debt in a simple systematic way.
➢ Three key principles to obtaining wealth.
➢ How to increase cash flow and ideas to create passive income.

Introduction
My Journey to a Land Filled with Milk and Honey

"No one can serve two masters. Either you will hate the one and love the other, or you will be devoted to the one and despise the other. You cannot serve both God and money."

~ Matthew 6:24

It began in 2006 when my husband and I moved from Sacramento, California to Atlanta, Georgia, to pursue our dreams of full-time real estate investing. At the time, we were doing well in the real estate arena. We owned seven investment properties, which we had accumulated over a two-year period in New York, Texas, and California, and were bringing in thousands of dollars in monthly rental income. We saw Georgia as a place we could continue our investment business because of the fairly low housing prices compared to other states like California.

We packed up the two dogs and piled boxes of possessions into the trailer, then started our journey to the *"land of milk and honey."* It was a beautiful drive across the country. We took our time and stopped in a few states along the way. However, from the time we left California, it seemed as if one thing after another went wrong with the investment properties—everything from air-conditioning repairs to a major water pipe break in a front yard. We

1

received emails from the property management companies about tenants' non-payment of rent, and from a few housing agencies requesting an enormous amount of repairs be done before they would pay their portion of the tenants' rent.

Neither my husband nor I had a job waiting for us in Atlanta, nor did we have plans for getting any. We thought that, with the amount of properties we had, we could live off the rental income. And our equity line of credit could be used to buy more properties. We would join a local church and get plugged into a ministry of our choosing. Life would be good.

So we thought…

Friends who recently moved to Atlanta were gracious enough to allow us to stay with them until we found a place to live, and within the first month of our arrival we started looking for a home. Another friend had contacted a real estate agent on our behalf to help us begin our search.

But the agent's lack of professional knowledge stood out when we gave her a description of our criteria and she constantly sent listings of homes that did not meet our requirements. However, we ignored the warning signs and continued working with her. She showed us properties in a sketchy area of the city, and although we'd done our homework researching crime rates at local police precincts, we, sadly ignored one officer's warning. He'd said he wouldn't live in the area because of the amount of crime.

Our desire for this new construction home that had an open floor plan, huge back yard, and view of downtown Atlanta won over the advice and information we had received about the dangers of the area. All we saw was the "perfect family home." And we wanted it to be ours, so we put in an offer to purchase.

Due to the quick low-documentation loan process, our offer was accepted, but before we closed on our home, we found two other investment properties in New York. We used our equity line of credit for a minimum down payment and received another low-documentation loan. We now had nine properties and were in the process of purchasing our primary home. Life *was* good.

Since we planned to buy more properties, I enrolled in school to get my real estate license.

We closed on what would be our primary home in January of 2007, and, within a few months, the real estate market started to plummet. In less than two years, all the properties were worth about half of what we owed.

Because of all of the investment property issues, our bank account was almost empty. At the same time, the volatile housing market forced the bank to stop our ability to borrow on the credit line.

After a few months, my husband found a minimum wage telemarketing job, which he hated. But at this point it didn't matter; we needed the money badly. I passed my real estate exam and had sold a few houses; however, we still didn't have enough money to pay the expenses on all our properties. To make ends meet, we started charging part of our monthly expenses on credit cards. You could say we had "way more month than money."

We accumulated over $130,000 in debt. This consisted of seven credit cards on which we owed a total of $39,000, an equity line of credit of $50,000, student loan debt of $38,000, and a car loan of over $10,000, not to exclude the mortgages on all ten properties. This totaled over a half million dollars.

For two years we struggled and allowed our financial circumstance to consume us mentally and emotionally. It robbed us of our peace and swiftly built a wedge between us. My husband and I argued constantly about money and were playing the blame game towards each other. We became more like roommates than soul mates, worrying about what to do with the properties because they were draining us "dry."

We finally talked and came to a point where we realized it could not be fixed in our own strength. We started to pray together, surrendering to God and asking for His guidance.

This was our turning point.

We attended a financial seminar and enrolled in an education class about managing money. We put a spending plan in place and listed all our revolving debt, along with the car and student loan debt, interest rates, and amounts. As we were paying off our debt in the beginning, we still struggled with not charging. For most of us, it takes time to stop a defeating habit, even when we are aware it's not good for us.

We continued to pay our primary bills on time, which consisted of the mortgage on the house we lived in, homeowners' insurance, car and life insurance, utilities, the car payment, student loan and credit card debt. We also consistently gave a financial offering to our local church.

My husband's paycheck and the money made when I sold a home paid for our necessities, then we put the rest toward the other debts, starting with the one that had the lowest balance. We stopped charging on all the credit cards. When we received our tax refund, it went to the debt, as did any other extra money we received. We stopped dining out and even cut back on drive-thru fast food. I cooked meals that would stretch for a day or two, such as spaghetti, chili, and beans and rice. It was so bad a friend nicknamed me "Burrito Girl" because I was eating frozen burritos every day for lunch while attending (real estate) school. We were determined to get out of this pit of debt.

In our marriage, I felt the love and unity being restored. God continued to meet our needs month by month. It was a faith walk. There were many times we didn't know if we would have enough money to pay our bills. God always provided.

Because of God's provision and our dedication and determination to the process, we were able to pay off $25,000 in credit card debt, $7,800 in student loan debt and $10,450 in automobile debt in twenty-four months.

Unfortunately, even while sticking to the plan and reducing our debt, we still found it difficult paying all ten mortgages each month. We eventually agreed that it was most important to take care of our primary household needs and we didn't have extra money to pay our additional mortgages due to tenants' non-payment of rent and the property management's excessive fees. We needed to let them go and start selling the properties.

Since we were upside down on most of the mortgages (owing more than the properties were worth) we hired real estate agents in the various cities and put the properties up as short sales. (A short sale is when the bank allows a property to be sold for less than what's owed. The lender then sends the seller a 1099 tax form for the difference between the purchase price and the balance of the loan.)

My husband and I made the decision to continue to let go and submit to the Lord, trusting Him for the outcome. But it didn't come without some bumps in the road.

The bank in New York was one of those bumps. They wouldn't accept the potential buyer's offer on two of the properties, so we couldn't sell the properties. We then tried giving them back to the bank—called a "deed in lieu" foreclosure—but they wouldn't work with us on that either.

Too add insult to injury, one of those properties needed repairs, and we didn't have the money. We had to winterize it instead, by wrapping insulation around the pipes, turning off the water and electricity, and boarding up the windows.

Then one day, as I was getting on the elevator to go to work, my husband phoned. He told me the New York fire department called saying that one of our houses had blown up! I suddenly felt a tightening in my chest; intense anxiety and fear came over me. I was in total shock. How could this happen? Was anyone hurt? He assured me that no one was hurt, which was such a relief. Despite our attempt to secure the property, someone had stolen the gas meter and that had caused the explosion. At this point we realized that we had no other recourse but to file bankruptcy.

As we went through the process, it was humiliating, humbling, yet at the same time we had a sense of peace. This entire experience brought us closer together and closer to God. Suddenly, the material possessions and the amount of money we made from owning properties was no longer our priority. We recognized that what started off as wise investments over time became our idols and we had gradually started chasing the money, rather than trusting and following the one who provided and led us to these opportunities...God. But now, as we started to make God a priority once again, our desires shifted. It was no longer real estate for personal gain we desired. It was helping His people in our surrounding area with their needs in an amazing new way.

During this time, my husband voiced a desire to help those in under-served communities like the one where we lived. In 2009, our community's average household income was $18,000 a year and serious strongholds plagued people's lives, such as alcohol, drugs, and prostitution. In 2010, he started a non-profit organization, Redemption & Advancement to help prevent incarceration and end recidivism for those living in under-served communities. The training helps individuals go from chaos to clarity and control in their lives, through a specialized cognitive thinking curriculum. Through it all, God gave us a sense of peace and calmness that was beyond measure as He continued to provide for us.

The lessons learned through our personal experiences helped my family and I live a more spiritually and financially free (fulfilling and joyful) life. Most importantly, they can help you and others overcome financial and spiritual obstacles as well. I am passionate about helping others recognize how the accumulation of debt literally keeps us enslaved and becomes a hindrance to us freely living out our God-given purpose in life.

Chapter 1

Money Mindset
"The rich rules over the poor and the borrower is a slave to the lender."
~Proverbs 22:7 NKJV

In this chapter you will learn about, and be able to apply the strategy necessary to go from operating in lack and "not enough" to a "more than enough; an abundance" mindset.

➢ Are you in a situation in life where you feel overwhelmed by the amount of bills you have each month?

➢ Does the debt continue to grow even though you are paying it off the best you can?

➢ Are you feeling stressed and worried about how you will come up with the money for your car, rent, or mortgage payments?

➢ Do you have little-to-no savings to pay for unexpected expenses that may come up?

➢ Are you tired of asking others to help you pay your monthly bills from time to time?

➢ Does it seem the more you try to figure out how to get out of debt, the more nothing seems to work?

➢ Because of the shame and guilt over your financial situation, do you isolate yourself?

➢ Maybe you and your spouse continue to argue over spending habits and you just can't seem to "get on the same page" as to how to budget your finances. You love each other, but the financial stress seems to be killing your marriage and pushing you further into debt.

I can relate to each situation and feelings of desperation because I have found myself in every one of those scenarios over the course of my life. The worst was when the real estate market started to decline in 2008, where I once again found myself back in debt.

I've felt hopeless, desperate, ashamed, and constantly argued with my husband every time we discussed our financial situation. I questioned my faith in God as well as my relationship with Him. I wondered how could someone who went to church every Sunday, served in multiple ministries, and worked hard at my job...could end up in this financial hell-hole once again?

This is when I took a good, hard look at my mindset behind my spending and how I viewed debt. The Lord revealed to me that we thought we were getting rich by buying all those properties, but we were actually becoming more and more of a slave to the lender. Proverbs 22:7 states "The rich rule over the poor, and the borrower is a slave lender."

As long as we owed someone else, whether it was the credit card or mortgage companies, that merchandise or property was not ours until we paid it off. The other important lesson we learned is that our core issue was not a lack of money, but the money habits and mindsets behind how we managed our money. What we focused on brought about the change in our circumstances. One of my favorite quotes is, *"What you focus on expands. So focus more on what you want, not what you do not want"*- Esther Jno-Charles

Once we stopped focusing on how little we had left over and how our bills kept piling up, and instead prayed and asked God for direction, increase in our finances to pay off the debt and trusted in His provision, we started to see the shift in our financial situation.

The exercise I am about to show you is crucial if you want to get out of debt and grow wealth.

Mark Twain says, *"The secret of getting ahead is getting started,"* so let's get started now...

I will teach you the strategies I personally used to:

➢ Bring awareness to your money mindset and how it is shaped by past experiences
➢ Understand and acknowledge that those were experiences and it does *not* have to be your current reality
➢ Identify your core values
➢ Create a new belief system that aligns with your core values

The change I believe you desire in your finances starts with your *thinking*, not your *circumstances*. Your circumstances are a byproduct of your mindset.

We must constantly ask ourselves, "What is the emotion or motive behind buying something?" Is it supportive of our core values, beliefs, and vision? Is this something that's needed now, or can we postpone it until we have more money? As a real estate consultant and investor who has learned some lessons the hard way, I know that when it comes to real estate, like most things in life, it is based on a cycle: what goes up must come down. When you are *not* in a hurry to purchase something you are less likely to be led by your emotions. If you are willing to wait, educate yourself, and position yourself for the opportune time you will reap the rewards. While others who "jumped on board" before truly understanding what they were signing up for and/or could not afford it, ended up with regret and heartache.

You must consider and evaluate what makes the best financial sense for you currently. It will save you a tremendous amount of stress in the future.

Now I realize that at any given moment something drastic can happen that could change someone's financial situation overnight, like an illness or accident. However, I still believe that even in those difficult circumstances, if we, over time, change our mindset and how we look at the circumstance, it will get better.

Emotions shouldn't rule financial decisions; our values and beliefs—our mindset—should.

***

So let's discover what our current mindset is and how it aligns with our core values.

Fear Driven vs. Faith Driven Mindsets

Which mindset below relates to where you are now?

Scarcity Mindset- This mindset is about believing that what you have is all you will *ever* have. You will live paycheck-to-paycheck because those are "the cards you were dealt in life."

Victim Mindset- This mindset is about believing that bad things *always* happen to you, and it is because of how you have been treated by other people that has determined the results in your life. Instead of taking ownership and responsibility for your circumstances.

Hoarding Mindset- This mindset is about believing you need to store up things because you *never* know when what you have will run out and you will need more.

Entitlement Mindset- This is the mindset that other people are obligated to take care of your needs. When they do not meet your expectations, you get upset.

Abundance Mindset- This is the mindset where you believe you are a joint heir with Jesus Christ and trust in His provision for your life. Therefore, you believe all your needs are met and what you have now is *not* all you will receive. You operate in overflow, believing that *everything* belongs to God and you are to be a good steward over all He has entrusted to you.

When you adopt the Abundance Mindset, you are driven by faith and not by fear like the *victim*, *hoarding, entitlement,* and *scarcity* mindsets. These fear-driven mindsets will cause you to feel stuck, frustrated, and unable to reach your goals and dreams. And the reality is that many times people have treated us unfairly, hurt us deeply and unfortunate circumstances have happened to us that have caused unforeseen hardships. And it is okay to be angry, upset, and hurt when those situations happen; just *don't* stay in that state, because the longer you allow yourself to entertain those thoughts and feelings the tougher it is to come out of that state of mind and overcome the circumstance. I recommend you always start with prayer, read the word of God and seek Him. You may also need to seek professional help from a counselor, doctor, coach or advisor. At the end of the day you may have a valid excuse for how life has "kicked you in the face" but the question remains: Are you going to rest in the excuses or "punch through" by focusing on the desirable results you deserve?

As was the case in my faith walk, you too are probably driven by fear when it comes to your financial life. Here is an exercise where I will teach you the strategies I personally used to transform my mindset from scarcity to abundance.

This exercise requires you to set aside time and be in a quiet space to reflect on the experiences growing up that formed your current mindset. Please don't skip or rush through these steps. It is crucial to your success, and taking time to invest in *you* could change your entire financial future.

It is best to set aside at least an hour of your time, grab your journal or notebook, favorite beverage and prepare mentally to do the work. You are worth it!

Let's look at your past and current money mindset.

Note: The exercise below can be used for all areas of your life such as career or relationships.

Awareness

Step 1: What things have you seen, heard, and experienced by parents, close relatives, and friends—your "influencers"—regarding money? For example: *"Money does not grow on trees," "You have to save for a rainy day," "Money is the root of all evil,"* et cetera.

Did your influencers use a spending plan regularly? Did they pay their bills on time? Did they talk to you about money?

What specific incidents do you recall? For example, were any utilities shut off? Were you faced with eviction? Or filed bankruptcy?

How old were you—old enough to form opinions or merely absorb the negative behavior demonstrated to you by this person? How did you react at the time outwardly or inwardly?

Next, take the time to reflect on the incident and feel the emotion behind the experience. How are you feeling toward that person or incident because of what took place?

Journal what was said, what you've seen, and how it made you feel inside.

Acknowledge & Understand
Step 2: Take some time to understand what you learned in Step 1 and how it may be affecting you today.

Do you find yourself repeating the same negative patterns? If so, in what ways? Identify those negative patterns affecting you currently in the area of your finances and the self-defeating results they are producing in your life.

These are experiences you were a part of, however they are not who you are. You get to *choose* today to let go of these past experiences and no longer allow them to define who you truly are. These influencers may be parents, relatives, a spouse—they did the best they knew how with the resources and knowledge they had at the time. It was their actions, not yours; you do not have to continue to own others' actions. You no longer have to be held hostage by your experiences.

Forgive
Step 3: Who is the person you may need to forgive? Could that someone be you? Either way, give yourself the freedom by forgiving. Write down their names.

I am choosing to forgive _____ (Insert person's name(s) _____ and be set free of resentment toward _____ (Insert person's name(s) _____

Prayer:

Father God, I need you to help me to let go of this hurt, bitterness, and/or anger I have been feeling toward _____ (Insert person's name(s) _____ because of what I experienced. I realize that those experiences are not my burden to carry. I do not have the capacity to fix his/her/their wrongs. I ask that you give me the heart and words to pray for them and release this burden I have been carrying so I can move forward in my life, free to pursue all You have in store for me to do and to be.

In Jesus' name. Amen.

Shift Your Focus

Step 4: In your journal, write down the person's name and the negative emotion you experienced.

After each negative emotion you felt based on the experience write the opposite next to it.

Examples:

Worry = Peace, Hope

Not enough = Overflow, Abundance, Prosperity

Anger = Joy, Love, Calmness

Resentment, Bitterness, Hurt = Forgiveness, Healing

Next, meditate on the new emotions and search biblical scriptures that reflect the emotions. *Example: Love, Forgiveness, Healing, Peace and Joy.*

The Real Truth

Step 5: Next, on a sheet of paper, write YOUR REAL TRUTH.

Example: "I have more than enough and operate out of an overflow in all areas of my life because I serve an abundant God with unlimited power. My Father is rich in all things, there is no lack in Him; therefore there is no lack in me".

"I choose to operate in love, joy and peace. I take control over my emotions and will not allow negative experiences to dictate my final outcome because greater is He that lives in me than He who is in the world. I can do all things through Christ who strengthen me"

Then place the sheet of paper somewhere you will be sure to see it *every* day. Repeat it out loud at least five times a day.

Repetition Is Key

I cannot stress enough the importance of recognizing and accepting the truth—that our experiences in life are not who we are and we must no longer allow them to shape our behavior.

For most of us, changing our mindset and forgiving does not happen instantly. This is a process that you will need to *repeat* each time those negative thoughts creep into your mind. Once the enemy sees he can no longer defeat you by controlling you emotionally and that you will no longer be held hostage by those self-sabotaging thoughts, he will leave you alone in that area of your life.

Just like when Jesus was tempted by the devil in the wilderness... Jesus resisted the trap of the enemy by uplifting the Lord and continued to trust in Him.

18

These days we are very fortunate to have the written word of God to read, speak, believe, and use to conquer the devil.

"The process to changing your mindset is like bathing, you don't do it once. It is a much needed daily habit."

- Darnyelle Jervey Harmon MBA, CEO of Incredible One Enterprises

There is one more important step, and that step is: we need to know and understand our core values in order to make the shift from scarcity to abundance mindset.

Belief System

The beliefs we have formulated in our minds dictate the decisions we make, which eventually give us the results we want or do not want in life.

What are your current beliefs regarding money/relationships/career? Write them in your journal.

Do you know your core values? Let us take time to identify your top seven.

Below are some examples. You can pick from the list and/or choose your own.

Write them in your journal.

Examples of Values

Integrity	Joy	Competence	Truth	Spirituality
Family	Strength	Loyalty	Gratitude	Prosperity
Perfection	Generosity	Community	Wealth	Creativity
Reliability	Money	Peace	Ambition	Humility
Determination	Faith	Authenticity	Pleasure	Being in Control
Love	Forgiveness	Freedom	Excellence	Encouragement
Hard work	Growth	Commitment	Service	Justice

Now pick your top four core values out of the seven mentioned and write them down. Make sure you know and are clear on at least these four top core values.

How to Make the Mental Shift
Thoughts + Values = Belief System (Aligning thoughts with/core values = Belief System)

Now that you have identified your current mindset and core values, it's important to determine if your current mindset is falling in line with your core values.

For most of us, the two are not in alignment, which is where the confusion, doubt, stress, and frustration occur. We want to be out of debt and manage our finances better, but our money mindset and habits keep us in debt. So how do we make the shift to the abundance/stewardship mindset we need? It starts with what we are feeding our minds. It is important that we feed our minds those things that line up with our core values.

For instance, as a follower of Christ, my values are focused around my belief that I am a child of God and He is my provider. I personally had to shift my belief that my finances are not solely based on my job or bank account, but on Christ. By constantly feeding my mind knowledge about God's provision through the word of God in the Bible, prayer, and biblical teachings I watch, listen to and read. This helps me to create a solid belief system, which transforms my mind and produces the abundance I experience in my daily life.

"Abundance starts in our thoughts way before we will see it manifest in our daily lives."

- unknown

Study Questions:

Write in your journal, the names of some people and/or things that you currently entertain that DO NOT line up with your core values.

Now name some people and/or things you currently entertain that DO line up with our core values.

Name some people and/or things you could incorporate into your life that DO line up with your core values to enhance your abundance mindset.

Examples: reading your Bible daily, listening to uplifting and positive videos, music, podcasts; joining groups of your same interest; volunteering with organizations that support a cause important to you.

Prayer:

Lord, you have given me a spirit of POWER, LOVE, and SELF-DISCIPLINE, therefore, fear cannot dwell here, and being timid is not a part of my character. I AM BOLD, COURAGOUS, and WISE. Lord, thank you for prosperity in all things, including good health as I continue to grow spiritually in You.

In Jesus' name. Amen.

Meditation:

"...my God shall supply all your need according to His riches in glory by Christ Jesus."

~ Philippians 4:19 NKJV

"For the Spirit God gave us does not make us timid, but gives us POWER, LOVE, and SELF-DISCIPLINE."

~ II Timothy 1:7 NIV

"The blessing of the Lord makes one rich and adds no sorrow with it."

~ Proverbs 10:22 NKJV

"Beloved, I pray that you may prosper in all things and be in health, just as your soul prospers."

~ 3 John 1:2 NKJV

"Blessed is the man who fears the Lord, who delights greatly in His commandments. His descendants will be mighty on the earth. The generation of the upright will be blessed. Wealth and riches will be in his house. And the righteousness endures forever. Unto the upright there arises light in the darkness; He is gracious and full of compassion, and righteous. A good man deals graciously and lends; he will guide his affairs with discretion. Surely he will never be shaken; the righteous will be in everlasting remembrances."

~ Psalm 112:1-6 NKJV

Chapter 2

TAKE Control of Your Financial Life
"Money is a great servant but a terrible master."
~ Francis Bacon

In 2017, the U.S. household debt balances were $12.73 trillion, a $149 billion increase from 2016. As of March 2017, 4.8% of outstanding debt was in some stage of delinquency and of the $615 billion delinquent debt, $426 billion was severely delinquent by 90 days or more.

According to the U.S. Census Bureau and Federal Reserve collectively, American households owe nearly $1 trillion in credit card debt, with an average interest rate of 18% in 2017. That averages out to $3,876 in interest only paid per household in three years! What could you have done with an extra $3,876?

Obviously, based on these statistics, the U.S. has fallen greatly into the temptation of greed and materialism in a capitalism-built society. These qualities have taken over us as a nation. It's time we no longer follow the path of the world's mentality of borrowing—which is destroying our nation—and follow the biblical principles found in this book to take back control over our finances.

The first thing you must do to master your money is *stop charging on your credit cards.*

This "buy now and pay later" mentality will get you so far into debt and cause you insurmountable amount of stress, worry, and heartache. You may already be experiencing the effect of the interest adding up quickly and the balances continuing to increase when paying only the minimal amount due. It is a trick by the enemy to get you trapped and feeling hopeless. I personally cut up my credit cards. I am not telling you to go to this extreme. You must make a decision based on your knowledge of your financial situation. But I will tell you this: If you do not take drastic measures to get of debt, starting with *not* using your credit cards, you will remain enslaved to your financial situation, which will, over time affect your health, personal relationships, and career.

And if you find yourself there right now, like I have many times before, this book will help guide you and give you the tools necessary to get completely out of debt no matter how much you owe!

Now, let's move on to the next most important step to becoming debt free by identifying the difference between a spending plan versus a budget, and why I prefer "Spending Plan."

A budget is like a diet…it doesn't work. It signifies restriction. However, a spending plan is you telling your money where it is going. It's when you take control and allocate where each dollar is going before it hits your bank account.

Do you have a spending plan *written* down? If so, are you following it?

If the answer is yes and the money plan is working for you, I still recommend reading through the exercise to find helpful tips you may want to implement. If you do not have a spending plan in place, welcome to a new beginning and a great start to financial freedom!

In order to take control of your finances, you must find out where you are currently.

If you were relocating to another state and you were driving your car to get there, one of the first things you would need to plug into your GPS (Global Positioning System) is your starting point. Where are you currently when it comes to your finances? If we don't know where we are currently, we cannot get to where we want to be.

Next, we would need to put our destination into the GPS. Where is it we are trying to get to? Now there are a few people who would just start driving to another state and figure it out as they went. Eventually they may make it there, but how much sooner do you think they would get there if they mapped it out versus trying to figure it out along the way?

How many of us handle our finances the same way? We navigate through life with no budget or spending plan, let alone written financial goals, and wonder why we remain stuck, repeating the same frustrating and stressful financial issues year after year.

Below is an exercise for you to put your spending plan in place. This will take approximately one to two hours. You will need to know all your expenses and income. If you do not have the time at this moment, pull out your calendar right now and schedule the time to get it done within the next week.

I recommend you find a quiet place, put on your favorite music, grab your favorite beverage, silence your phone, and invest in yourself by putting in the work to get it done.

Depending on how simple or detailed you would like to be, you can use a sheet of paper or use spreadsheet software to do your written spending plan.

Step 1: List ALL your monthly income
(including alimony, child support, bonuses, etc.)

Step 2: List ALL outgoing expenses

What about those expenses that vary in cost each month, such as utilities, gasoline, etc.? Review the cost for each item during the prior three to six months and use the average amount.

Example: Category: Electricity for October $109, November $155 and December $175. Then total the three months of electricity expenses, which is $439, divide by 3 = $146 is the average electricity expense for those three months. You would put $146 on spending plan under electricity.

Most utility companies offer a fixed payment plan based on your yearly average usage. Also, shop around with different utility companies to get the best rate. If you find a better rate someplace else, negotiate with your current company to see if they will match the lower rate, instead of you having to switch and your current company losing an existing customer. Once you have the average amount, put it down under the proper category.

Spending Plan Guidelines
Cost of Living Categories

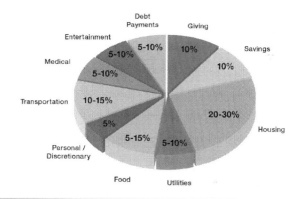

Cost of Living Spending Plan Categories

Housing = 20-30% rent/renters' insurance/mortgage/mortgage insurance/property taxes

Utilities = 5-10%- phone/electricity/gas/internet/cable/water/trash

Food = 5-15%- groceries (including household/personal hygiene)

Personal & Discretionary = 5%- haircuts/nails/hobbies

Transportation = 10-15%- car payment/car insurance/parking fees/maintenance/public transportation/taxi (Uber or Lyft)

Medical/Dental/Vision = 5-10%- healthcare premiums/co-payments/medications

Entertainment- 5-10%- movies, concerts, amusements parks, etcetera.

Debt payments = 5-10%- many people find that their spending plan is quite tight because their monthly debt payments are closer to 25% of their net income.

Giving = 10% - Be a CHEERFUL giver— give to your local church and/or favorite charities

Savings = 10%- save money for expenses that do not occur every month, as well as for your future. Then you will have a little extra available when you need it.

All these cost of living percentages are based on using net income

I realize for some of you, following this chart in your current financial situation seems next to impossible. That's okay. This is not a guide that must be followed precisely, but instead a starting point for balancing your spending plan. Remember: You are the financial manager of what God has entrusted to you. My objective in this book is to help you discover the power within you—no matter where you find yourself financially—to take control of your money and provide the tools, resources, and wisdom that God gave me to help get you out of debt, increase your income, and live the life you crave!

What would it look like for you, and how would it feel if your debt payments were at 0% with a surplus?

It can happen—with prayer, mindset shift, discipline in following your spending plan, and expanding your vision.

What to do when your income varies

It can be difficult when you are trying to put a spending plan in place and follow it each month, but your income fluctuates. I have experienced this challenge as a real estate agent. Many times, months went by before I was paid the commissions on a sale. Since my husband operates a non-profit, his income also varies month to month. So we had to come up with a way to consistently manage our money.

If you earn by commission only, like I did, it is important not to deceive yourself into thinking you have a surplus when you take in a large chunk of cash. Instead, figure out your annual income and divide that amount by twelve, then develop your monthly spending plan based on that amount. If I was only halfway into the year and did not want to base my income off last year's earnings, I would take the previous six months of my income divide by six and use that amount as my average monthly income.

Open a separate savings account title it "income account" and deposit your income into it when you get paid. Then, each month, transfer the monthly income average out of your "income account" into your checking account to cover your monthly expenses.

According to Crown Ministries, this method will allow surplus funds to accumulate in the income account to cover budgeted expenses during months of lower income. It is not hoarding. It is planning according to *Proverbs 6:6-8: "Go to the ant, you sluggard! Consider her ways and be wise, which, having no captain, overseer or ruler, provides her supplies in the summer and gathers her food in the harvest."*

Automation Is Key

It is one of the best ways to pay bills, save, and give.

We have all heard the saying, "Work smarter not harder."

And we all have a ton of things going on in life—family, work, charitable activities, and so on—so it is challenging and can be overwhelming to do it all. Most of us do not want to sit down, pay our bills, place stamps on the envelopes, and mail them off.

You don't have to do that anymore. Instead, set up as many of your monthly bills on auto-pay as possible. You can do this through your bank, or companies that are set up to accept payments online via auto-pay on their individual websites. (Note: I prefer to set it up on my bank's website because I can stop the automatic payment at any time before the scheduled payment date.)

Automation is KEY because it minimizes the time spent managing your finances and will ensure:
➢ No late payments
➢ No more time spent paying each bill manually

➢ No more writing checks, and spending money on checks and postage

(Note: Set up an automatic notification through your bank to alert you when your balance drops below a specific amount.)

However, do not rely on this method as your primary way to track your finances. Instead, use it as an additional mechanism to monitor finances.

➢ Make sure to check your account frequently (at least once a week) to keep up to date on the current balance and make sure there are no fraudulent charges.

➢ Be consistent in following your spending plan; tracking your spending is crucial to success.

Savings Account

In order to grow your savings, set up an automated "payday" for yourself, so on that day, a specified amount will be transferred from your checking into your "Just In Case" saving account.

I use the term "Just in Case Fund", rather than "Emergency Fund" because it's important not to tie negativity to your money or any other areas of your life. "Just in Case Fund" is for any unexpected circumstances that arises.

Since certain expenses vary month to month, whenever the actual bill amount is less than what you have written down in your spending plan, put the extra money in your "Just In Case Fund" to increase your savings.

Giving Automatically

Giving should be a priority. It is important to living a wealthy and abundant life. It allows us the opportunity to give back some of what God has given us. You might be in a position where your budget is so tight you feel you can't afford to give, but the truth is you can't afford not to give. Remember, it's not equal giving; it's equal sacrifice. (Malachi 3:6-8)

Spending Systems

The system you use is important; however, the most important thing is finding a system that works best for you to manage spending and following it consistently.

Now, let's look at which spending method will serve you best.

Cash Only

Pros- instantly aware of how much you have left to spend.

Cons- it is hard to track your itemized spending. You must keep all receipts or use one of the tracking apps that will help you track your expenses.

Cash cannot be replaced if lost or stolen.

There are bills that must be paid online or via check.

Debit Card only

Pros- a great way to track itemized spending because you have a record of the purchase through the bank. You do not have to worry about losing your cash.

Cons- Some people tend to spend more because the physical cash is not leaving their hands.

If you do not consistently track your expenses online, it can be easy to over-spend and be charged overdraft fees.

Cash and Debit Card

(Pay most bills online, withdraw the allocated amount of cash according to your spending plan for dining out, entertainment, personal care, groceries, etc.)

Pros- This will help avoid over-spending on the majority of daily expenses because you can physically see how much you have left over to spend and how much you are spending.

Cons- It is important to keep receipts for tracking expenses, especially for tax purposes.

Choosing Your Spending and Savings Tracking System

As you are reading this book, there are probably lots of other efficient tracking systems available because of how fast technology evolves. Therefore, I recommend researching online to see what other tracking tools are available before choosing a system.

The system and/or software you use is important; however, the most important principles are to use a system that works for you and make managing your system a weekly habit.

When trying a new tracking system, prepare to spend two to three *hours* to set up accounts and two to three *months* to get comfortable using the software.

Set aside the time, a quiet place, with your favorite music and beverage, and dedicate yourself to learning the software.

Here are a few options to consider:

Quicken.com: Personal finance tool to manage your money

Mvelopes.com: Track bills, manage spending plan

Mint.com: Manage money, pay bills, and track credit score

YNAB.com- You Need A Budget: Personal finance tool providing helpful budgeting tips as well as helping you manage your money.

Expensify.com: Tracks and files expenses. It allows users to take a photograph of a receipt which is then saved and categorized in Expensify. It also creates expense reports.

Please keep in mind that as God starts to bless you by increasing your income, you may start to become slothful in following your plan and tracking where the money is going, because you have a surplus at the end of the month. However, please heed this warning: This is even more of a reason to stay committed to your plan, because God is increasing your income to accelerate your debt elimination and in doing so creating the freedom to live out your purpose without the restraints of debt.

Stewardship Exercise

This exercise will help you find out what you treasure most and in what categories you can decrease your expenses. First print the last three months of your bank statements.

Using different color highlight markers, highlight each category with a different color marker and then add up each category separately for each month. Now review how you have been spending your money in each category and whether you are staying within your budgeted amount.

Example: Category- Groceries for October $399, November $655 and December $705.

You want to do the following exercise for the four areas listed below to find out what you value most and help you identify areas you may want to reduce your spending.

One- Groceries

Two- Eating out

Three- Merchandise shopping: clothes, shoes

Four- Giving

➤ After completing this stewardship exercise, do you see areas where you are overspending?

Most of us overspend in the eating out or groceries categories.

➤ Do you feel it would benefit you to decrease your spending in a particular area and allocate more money to another category in your spending plan?

➤ Are you satisfied with the amount of money you allocated to giving?

➢ Do you feel you are being a good steward over God's resources?

If your answer is *yes*, that's great! If instead you see room for improvement in managing spending, congratulate yourself for taking the steps to becoming a better steward over your finances and know you are on your way to living a life free of financial burden and despair.

Debt Elimination Strategy

There are various methods to paying off debt. Here is the method we used to help pay off our debt. We first started by listing all our revolving debt such as credit card(s), personal loan(s), student loan(s), etcetera, on a large poster board in order from the lowest to highest balance with creditor's names. If a particular debt had a specific deadline date such as "six months same as cash debt" or "balloon payment" we included the due date. Those debts became priority based on their due dates to prevent the total interest over the duration of loan being called due by the specified deadline.

The interest rate became a concern for us only when there were debts with similar payoff balances. In this case we would pay the debt with the highest interest rate over the debt with the lower interest to avoid paying more interest over time.

As you list out your revolving debt on the poster board those self-sabotaging, limiting beliefs will try to creep in your mind such as "You will never be able to get out of all this debt.". Use this "Debt

Elimination Board" as your "plan of attack!" Remembering "What you focus on expands" and immediately start to envision how your life will be once the debt is paid off. The freedom you will gain by having more time, more options, not to mention more cash flow!

As we started to apply extra funds toward the lowest amount of debt *first* we didn't focus on how little the amount was that we were able to pay on the debt. Instead we celebrated the fact that we had the extra funds to put on the bill and were choosing to direct funds toward paying down our debt. We eventually paid it off completely by applying the additional funds consistently each month to the balance. Then we crossed out the debt on our board and put the payoff date next to it. Next we took the total amount we were paying previously on lowest debt and added it to the *second* lowest bill. We repeated this process which helped us gain momentum as we continued to pay off our debt.

Debt Elimination Board

Creditor's Name	Total Balance	Minimum Monthly Payment	Additional Funds Applied to Debt	Total Monthly Payment	Payoff Date
Credit Card 1	$90	$20	$70	$90	(insert date)
Credit Card 2	$300	$25	$90	$115	(insert date)
Credit Card 3	$6900	$120	$115	$235	(insert date)
Student Loan	$23,000	$320	$235	$555	(insert date)
Car Payment	$26,000	$350	$555	$905	(insert date)

Source: Fictitious data, for illustration purposes only

Most of you may already be familiar with this process of debt elimination. If you already know about this method that's great. The question to ask yourself is are you consistently applying it?

I know from experience there will be moments when you stray from your plan, don't allow yourself to stay stuck feeling guilty. Instead recognize the "not so good choice" and move forward deciding that you will make better money choices starting today.

What happens far too often is that we don't see the *instant* benefits of our hard work and we give up just when the result we desire is about to happen.

Student Loans
Student loan debt leaves Americans with an outrageously high and stressful financial burden. The economic impact it causes to borrowers and their families is insurmountable.

According to the Federal Reserve, in 2017 student loan debt in the U.S. totaled $1.48 trillion. The number of Americans carrying student loan debt is approximately $44.2 million and the average debt per borrower is estimated to be $37,000.

However, there is good news for those who may qualify for the PSLF (Public Service Loan Forgiveness) Program. According to studentaid.ed.gov, this program forgives the remaining balance on your Direct Loans after you have made 120 qualifying monthly payments under a qualifying repayment plan while working full-time for a qualifying employer. It's important to note that only payments made after October 1, 2007, can be counted toward the PSLF.

Qualifying employment for the PSLF Program is not about the specific job that you do for your employer. Rather, it is about who your employer is. Employment with the following types of organizations most likely qualifies for PSLF:

➢ Government organizations at any level (federal, state, local, or tribal)
➢ Not-for-profit organizations that are tax-exempt under Section 501(c)(3) of the Internal Revenue Code
➢ Other types of not-for-profit organizations that are not tax-exempt under Section 501(c)(3) of the Internal Revenue Code, if their primary purpose is to provide certain types of *qualifying public services*.

You will want to complete and submit an Employment Certification and Public Service Loan Forgiveness Form, which you can obtain for free at studentaid.ed.gov. In addition, the U.S. Department of Education's loan service is a great resource that will help you, free of charge, with your student loan needs.

Cash in on the Tax Benefits
Do not forget to deduct the interest from your student loan(s) when you file taxes.

Repayment Strategy
When repaying your loan, put extra money toward the principal each time you make a payment. Include a note with your payment explaining that the extra amount is to go toward reduction of principal, otherwise the processor may apply it to the accruing interest on the loan.

As of 2008, you can pay off as much of your loan as you want without penalty, whether they are private or public loans. You can request a short payment schedule. These things will help save you money, because you will accrue less interest.

If you have multiple loans, consider consolidating them into one loan with a lower interest rate that would allow for more of your monthly payment to go toward paying down the principal. Whether you have multiple loans or one, refinancing to a lower rate can be very beneficial to you paying off your loan sooner.

Again studentaid.ed.gov is a free government resource that is willing and able to help with your student loan needs. Also, I have listed several ideas on how to increase your cash flow to accelerate your debt pay off in the "Shift Your Elimination Debt Efforts into Overdrive" chapter.

Chapter 3

Shift Your Debt Elimination Efforts into Overdrive

"However difficult it may be to accept situations we find ourselves in, one must understand that moments such as this give us the possibility for radical change in our behavior."
~ *Paul Coelho*

Do you have a desire to have RADICAL change in your financial life? It takes RADICAL ACTION, being uncomfortable, prudent, determined, and dedicated. It takes going to the extreme to cut cost and increase your cash flow. This may mean taking on more hours at your full-time job, working an additional part-time job temporarily, or using your talents, gifts, passion, and expertise to create a second source of income, while maintaining your full-time job.

Here are some ways to make additional income:

Become a local transportation driver - providing transportation to individuals or delivering packages during the hours you are not working your full-time job.

Personal or Virtual Assistant services - performing administrative, technical or social media assistance to clients from home or remotely.

Caregiver part-time - a paid helper who regularly takes care of a child, elderly or disabled person.

Pet sitting- there are pet owners who need pet walking and/or watching their pets while at work or on vacation.

Sell new or gently used items online- sell items around the house that you are not using or find items at a discount (local garage sales, flea markets, antique auctions) and resell. Selling items from home is not only a way of making more money, but decluttering your surroundings also.

Is there a certain skill set you could use to help others? Do you speak a foreign language? Are you good at an academic subject such as math, reading, S.T.E.M (Science, Technology, Engineering, Mathematics)? Tutoring services are a high-demand business. Offer in-person or online classes, and if you help a group of students rather than just one, you can maximize your impact, time, and profit.

Start a home-decorating service, give creative writing workshops, provide bakery services such as custom cakes or cupcakes, start a web design business, become an IT consultant, start a free-lance photography business, or teach a photography class if you have talents in those areas.

For each one of these opportunities listed, there are businesses you can hire that will, for a fee, automatically connect you with people who need your services, using mobile apps. Utilize the internet to research available companies on the specific topic of your interest.

An immediate way to generate more cash to pay off debt would be to work overtime at your current job. However, please keep in mind that when you choose to work overtime, it will, most likely, cost you more than it will help overall. Once you add up the taxes the employer takes out, time away from home and family, at the end you may merely break even.

Another way that does not require more hours and generates more cash flow is to find a roommate or rent out rooms. For obvious reasons, getting a roommate or renting out a room will most likely be a temporary solution for most, because of the lack of privacy and space.

When finding a roommate to split rent and housing bills or renting out a room, be sure to do a criminal background check and require referrals from prior landlords. Check credit score and independently confirm their employment.

Or, maybe it's time to downsize in the area of housing and transportation. Are you in a location where you can use public transportation to save money on gas to and from work? Should you move into a place that is lower in rent or mortgage? That's a decision only you can make based on what you believe is best for you in your current circumstances and keeping in mind that it takes a sacrifice of your current comfort to get where you ultimately want to be in the near future.

Start Your Own Business
The information provided thus far was to help you accelerate paying off your debt. These

suggestions are perfectly fine for the beginning stages of paying down your bills and temporary sacrifices to get out of debt sooner. They are not necessarily a way to create financial wealth for you and your family.

A way to create financial freedom is entrepreneurship. Why not start a business around your talents and/or gifts? Develop a business plan, research and discover creative ways to build a successful business that provides passive income and multiple streams of income.

Passive income is when you produce something one time that continues to generate cash flow for you, with little to no continual work.

Multiple streams of income is when you have cash flow coming from several different sources.

I have listed in the next section some ideas to stop trading your time for money, become debt free, and increase your cash flow doing what you love.

Ideas to Creating Passive Income & Multiple Streams of Income

Everyone has a story, something impactful that has happened in their life. It could be a tragedy they overcame, a significant victory they never thought was possible...maybe it is a combination of both. Either way, the question to ask yourself is: How could someone's life be drastically impacted for the better by me sharing my story? You could do this in a few ways.

Here are a couple of examples:

You can write and publish a book, and make passive income every time someone purchases it. Become a combination of *published author and professional speaker*. It is a great way to reach more people with your message and to also create multiple streams of income, which is an important key to financial freedom.

I recognize that public speaking is one of the greatest fears for a majority of us. However, to help conquer that fear and perfect sharing your story so it is impactful to others, I recommend joining Toastmasters International. This organization provides, support, encouragement, guidance, resources in a non-judgmental atmosphere, which allows you to grow in skill and confidence.

➢ Create an Online Business providing a service or product.

Do you speak a foreign language? Are you an artist? Are you a musician? Share your gift by *creating a "How-To" online course* on things people are interested in learning. Record it once, market online, and continue to make money.

➢ Affiliate Marketing

Affiliate Marketing is a way for a company to sell its products by signing up individuals or companies ("affiliates") who market the company's products for commission.

If you have a strong social media presence, think about *providing affiliate marketing* for a particular product you think your social media followers would like to buy.

> ➤ Collaborate and form business partnerships called a Joint Venture

According to Wikipedia, a "Joint Venture is a business entity created by two or more parties, generally characterized by shared ownership, shared returns and risks, and shared governance."

Are there businesses out there that complement what you are doing and/or add value to the people you are serving? Why not collaborate with them to reach more of the people you are currently serving and to make a greater impact by the added value the partnership could possibly provide?

Invest in Real Estate

I believe investing in real estate is still one of the best ways to create financial wealth. Two ways are to buy properties and rent them out, creating passive income, or buy properties that require fix up and resale. There are multiple ways to invest and profit in real estate. I've learned a lot after 15 years of investing in real estate and made a generous amount of money in this profession. The hardships my husband I experienced during the housing market crash in 2008-2010 left me better, not bitter. The wisdom I gained about not over-leveraging funds is priceless, along with having learned when the most opportune time is to buy investment property.

Beware of becoming impatient and moving too quickly to grow your business. It's important to continue to ask God for His wisdom every step of the way.

I realized the hard way that debt—whether we use the terms credit, loan, or interest-free for a certain amount of time—are just ways in which we become the borrower and, in turn, the slave, indebted to the world system. However, as we grow in our knowledge, discipline and trust in God we will make wiser decisions.

"The rich rule over the poor, and the borrower is a slave to the lender."

~ Proverbs 22:7 NIV

God already knows our heart's desires, and promises to provide for us even more than He does for all the other species of this world. However, we have to be willing to let go and put our trust in Him rather than in the wants and desires of our flesh. When we seek Him first, and delight ourselves in Him, we will experience His goodness and faithfulness.

"Delight yourself in the Lord and He will give you the desires of your heart."

~ Psalm 37:4-6 ESV

When someone GIVES something to you, it's yours. You don't have to borrow it, or pay it back over time.

God wants to do so much in and through us, but the heavy burden of debt restrains us from being able to receive all He has for us. However, when we put our focus back on God and continue to seek Him through prayer and reading the Bible, He promises all these things shall be added on to us. God is faithful. The question to stop and ask yourself is: "Will I trust Him in every aspect of my life including my money?"

Prayer:
Dear Father God, thank you for being my Provider, my Refuge, and my Redeemer. I ask that you continue to guide my steps as I put my trust in you. Lord, I thank you for providing me the wisdom I need to be a great steward over my finances and all that you have entrusted to me. Lord, I ask you to pour out so many blessings that I cannot contain them all, and guide me to use them to invest in your Kingdom. You are sovereign Lord and I know that you will supply *all* my needs according to your riches in Christ Jesus. Amen.

Meditation:
"Therefore, I tell you, do not worry about your life, what you will eat or drink; or about your body, what you will wear. Is not life more important than food, and body more important than clothes? Look at the birds of the air; they do not sow or reap or store away in barns, and yet your Heavenly Father feeds them. Are you not much more valuable than they? Who of you, by worrying, can add a single hour to his life? And why do you worry about clothes? See how the lilies of the field grow? They do not labor or spin. Yet I tell you that not even Solomon in all his splendor was dressed like one of these. If that is how God clothes the grass of the field, which is here today, and, tomorrow, is thrown into the fire, will He not much more clothe you, O you of little faith? So do not worry,

saying, *"What will we eat?"* or *"What shall we drink?"* or *"What shall we wear?"* For the pagans run after all these things, and your Heavenly Father knows that you need them."*

~ Matthew 6:25-34 NIV

"Let no debt remain outstanding, except the continuing debt to love one another, for he who loves his fellowman has fulfilled the law."

~ Romans 13:8 NIV

"But seek ye first his Kingdom and his righteousness, and all these things will be given to you as well. Therefore, do not worry about tomorrow, for tomorrow will worry about itself. Each day has enough trouble of its own."

~ Matthew 6:33 NIV

Chapter 4

What Are the Most Important Keys to Wealth?
The First Most Important Key to Wealth

"If any of you lack wisdom, he should ask God,
who gives generously to all without fault, and it will be given to him"
~ James 1:5 NIV

Most would say that gaining more money is the most important component in obtaining wealth. And although money is important, it is not the *most* important thing, because wealth is much more than finances alone.

Henry David Thoreau says *"Wealth is the ability to fully experience life"*

Everyone's definition of wealth varies because we each have our own perspective of what wealth looks like in our individual lives.

However, one thing I realized while researching wealth and abundance is that they have very similar meanings such as plentiful, "more than enough"; and overflow.

My personal definition of wealth is being in great health, having a healthy marriage and family that is functioning in an overflow of love, joy, kindness and generosity. We are following Christ by fully walking in our purpose, lacking for nothing and operating in an abundant overflow of valuable resources to further help advance God's Kingdom.

The first most important key to wealth is getting WISDOM.

Why wisdom?

"...Wisdom is protection even as money is protection, but the (excellent) advantage of knowledge is that wisdom shields and preserves the lives of its possessors."

~ Ecclesiastes 7:12 AMP

Although money is a tool that provides protection along with other things, it is also temporary. For most people it only takes one drastic situation to wipe out a person's entire savings, not to mention the value of currency going up and down.

However, wisdom and knowledge are things no one can take from you. They are available to all of us and we can continue to build on them. You receive wisdom in many different ways. One of the most common is what you learn through your experiences in life. Those life lessons that help you to make wiser decisions moving forward. Or maybe it comes from a coach or mentor who shares the same pitfalls you experienced, similar to what I am doing in this book. Then, of course, there is the knowledge you receive from your own research or courses and classes you've taken.

However, I believe the most important and powerful wisdom given to those who believe in Jesus is the revelation of Him speaking directly to you. There are times when I seek God in prayer asking for His wisdom and guidance in a certain circumstance, and I hear the Holy Spirit speak to me. It's this soft, gentle voice speaking to my heart. In order for me to clearly hear from Him, I first must quiet the noise around me, and all the random thoughts going on in my mind. I intentionally have to seek out a quiet location and opportune time. It could be early in the morning before anyone else in the house is awake, late at night when they are sleep, or alone in the car.

Everyone's lifestyle varies, so you find what works best for you. There also are those times when I can't wait for an opportune time. I need a word from Lord quickly I have learned how to block out the external and internal noise, be still, and listen. The beauty of the Lord is that He is always available to hear from us and willing to answer our prayers.

Wisdom is given in many different forms. It helps us to be able to discern and make better choices on what we should or should not do.

Let's take a look at Solomon, son of David in the Bible, book of Chronicles

In the book of II Chronicles 1:7, God appeared to Solomon son of David and said to him, *"Ask! What I shall give you?"* In other words, "Ask what you would like." Solomon could have asked for anything at all, however how Solomon responded was a reflection of his heart. Solomon asked God for wisdom and knowledge. He had a strong desire to lead God's people in excellence and he knew this calling would require God's direction and guidance.

In II Chronicles, it goes on to state God had favor upon Solomon. Solomon was a man who delighted himself in the Lord. He was a man after God's own heart. He made God and God's people his priority. God was pleased with Solomon's response, so much so that He not only granted Solomon the wisdom and knowledge he asked for, but also gave him riches, possessions, honor, and glory. Solomon reigned over Israel and was given so much wealth that it says in II Chronicles 1:15 that the kings made silver and gold as common as stones!

Please understand I am not saying that if you ask God for wisdom, instead of financial increase, you will automatically receive an overflow of both. God is the giver and He decides what, when, and how much of all things He gives. I do believe He has given all of us wealth to receive and it will look different for each of us.

Solomon's priority was to seek God and serve Him well.

Solomon asked for wisdom and God gave him wisdom and financial wealth.

Solomon ended up becoming one of the richest men in all the Bible.

Key Characteristics of Solomon, son of David:
➢ Grateful- Solomon recognized how merciful God had been in his father David's life and the Lord's loving kindness toward him. *II Chronicles 1:8*

➤ Humble- Solomon knew he needed God's wisdom and knowledge to effectively operate as king over His people. *II Chronicles 1:10*

➤ Serving God was his first priority- Solomon was not all about money but serving God's people with excellence. *II Chronicles 1:11; Matthew 6:33*

"If any of you lacks wisdom, he should ask God, who gives generously to all without fault, and it will be given to him."
~ James 1:5 NIV

God says that if we ask for wisdom he will freely give it. However, I believe the first important step is that we prepare ourselves to receive.

➤ Pray- Ask God to show you those hardened areas in your heart where the pain or hurt has turned to bitterness, or self-righteousness has set in. Are there areas of unforgiveness trapped in your heart? This is the time to repent and ask God to heal you and deliver you in those areas.

➤ Recognize how merciful God is in your life— that none of us are perfect, but we serve a God who is...Thank Him for His loving kindness toward you. Reflect on the goodness of God in your life. Having and maintaining a grateful heart is an important ingredient to obtaining wealth.

➢ Humility- continual dependence on God. Live a life of worship and continual dependence on God. *"With man this is impossible, but with God all things are possible."* -Matthew 19:26 NIV

Money comes; money goes, but no one can ever take your wisdom away. Instead of our primary focus being on money, focus on seeking God's wisdom through prayer and mediating on His word.

I gained a better understanding of money and where true provision comes from going through the storm of losing the financial wealth than I did while obtaining all the many investment properties.

Study Questions:
Do you believe wisdom is more important than money? If so, in what ways is wisdom more important than money?

Are you currently trusting more in your possessions (money, job, spouse, etc.) than God?

Based on what you read what are three things you will do starting tomorrow to shift your focus more on God than money?

Do you recall a time in the past when you were going through a financial storm and God provided for you? Write it down.

What about the experience made you know it was God? Write it down.

Based on what you read, what three things will you do differently, starting tomorrow, in becoming financially free?

Prayer:

Father God, your Word says that if I lack wisdom to ask You, and You will generously give it to me. I ask that you give me your wisdom; not as the world giveth, but in Your way, Lord, so that I may gain Your knowledge and wisdom, to follow You and do Your will. I stand on Your promise, the Living Word, and believe You are giving me wisdom, insight and revelation.

In Jesus' name. Amen.

Meditation:

"Blessed are those who find wisdom, those who gain understanding, for she is more profitable than silver, and yields better return than gold. She is more precious than rubies; nothing you desire can compare with her. Long life is in her right hand; in her left are riches and honor. Her ways are pleasant ways, and all her paths are peace. She is a tree of life to those who take hold of her; those who hold her fast will be blessed."

~ Proverbs 3:13-18 NIV

"Command those who are rich in this present world not to be arrogant nor put their hope in wealth, which is so uncertain, but put their hope in God, who richly provides us with everything for our enjoyment."

~ 1 Timothy 6:17 NIV

The scripture 1 Timothy 6:17 talks about material possessions, which come and go. We never want to tie our identity to the things we possess, for when those things disappear, so will our identity. But instead, we should fix our identity on Jesus and being joint heirs with Him.

"Seek ye first the Kingdom of God and His Righteousness, and all these things shall be added on to you."
~ Matthew 6:33 NKJV

"And you shall remember the Lord your God, for it is He who gives you power to get wealth, that He may establish His covenant, which He swore to your fathers, as it is this day.
~Deuteronomy 8:18 NKJV

"Both riches and honor come from You, And You reign over all. In Your hand is power and might; In Your hand it is to make great And to give strength to all.
~ I Chronicles 29:12 NKJ

Chapter 5

The Second Most Important Key to Wealth
"The earth is the Lord's, and everything in it,
the world, and all who live in it."
~ Psalm 24:1 NIV

The second most important key to wealth is good stewardship. Stewardship is the careful and responsible management of something entrusted to one's care. It is expressed by our obedience in how we manage everything God has given us, recognizing that it all belongs to Him.

You and I are the money managers, financial stewards over the money God has entrusted to us. However, we often confuse management with ownership. Stewardship is not ownership. It's important to remember that all we have belongs to the Lord.

A good steward recognizes that God is their Provider, and constant prayer is essential in focusing their actions on His Will. He is all-knowing and everything comes from Him. That is why it is so important to seek His guidance regarding your finances.

As author Randy Alcorn stated, *"Whenever we think we are owners, it's a red flag. We should be thinking like stewards, investment managers, always looking for the best place to invest the Owner's money."*

As your trust in the Lord grows, you will become more aware of His provision and guidance. As you follow His direction, your financial circumstance will start to improve. Our God is sovereign and has the ability to change your financial circumstance at any moment.

For instance, this week God could have you meet someone who presents an opportunity for you to benefit financially. It would impact not only you, but the lives of those close to you. For example: In 2008, I had recently passed my real estate exam and it was challenging getting leads to those who wanted to purchase or sell real estate. My husband and I were struggling to pay our bills and had piles of debt. However, we were still faithfully giving and serving at our local church.

We had recently moved to Georgia, and homes around us had gone through foreclosure. On this particular day, my husband happened to be outside in our front yard. The construction company the bank hired to fix up the homes in our neighborhood for resale was outside too. The manager for the construction company and my husband started a conversation regarding the homes, and my husband mentioned I was a real estate agent. The manager took my information and passed it on to the bank. The bank manager called me for an interview. After the interview, the bank hired me to be the listing agent for all four houses right next door. The earnings from the sale of the homes were thousands of dollars in commissions, and it couldn't have come at a more opportune time. I truly believe God orchestrated that opportunity to bless our family and provide for our financial needs. That one opportunity created even more over time. God is so good. Our job is to trust Him and believe He will do what He says in His word.

Another very important attribute of a good steward is being generous with your money as well as your time.

I believe in consistently giving a portion of your income to your local church and/or charitable organization to whom you feel led to give by the Holy Spirit.

I do not believe anyone has to give a specific percentage. Instead as you consistently give with gratitude because of all God has given to you, recognizing how blessed you are, overtime you cannot help but continue to increase your giving.

"Honor the Lord with your firstfruits of all your increase; So your barns will be filled with plenty, And your vats will overflow with new wine"

~ Proverbs 3:9-10

Giving shifts your focus from *self* to sharing with others what God has entrusted to you, and in turn using it to bless others. When you give, it helps break the bondage of living in a *lack* mentality. Which, remember, is fear driven. Giving is the antidote to crushing the scarcity/lack mentality and opening opportunity for abundance to enter.

Please don't confuse abundance with mere money. Abundance is the freedom of living and depending on God, knowing and trusting He is and will continue to provide in all areas of your life with more than enough, in areas such as your health, finance, relationships and career.

As you give, your heart is being propelled toward God's will and His people. The more we freely and wisely give, the deeper our soul desires to help others.

When you shift your mindset from yourself, you begin to realize the privilege God has given to you to give to others and help impact someone else's life by meeting a need or desire. This is one of the beginning stages to understanding how wealthy you already are.

A critical component to giving is your motive behind giving.

Do you give with a sincere heart or is it begrudgingly or out of obligation? If there are areas you give, but begrudgingly, start by confessing it to the Lord and asking Him to reveal to you why. It may not be an area to which the Lord is leading you to give, or more than likely you are operating in fear and lack. Somewhere down the line, you have drifted from a place of gratitude in your life. If that is the case, it's okay because most of us, if we are honest with ourselves, have given out of obligation many times throughout our journey in life. The important point is that we recognize, confess, and take the necessary steps to correct it.

One of the things I do is write down each day something for which I am grateful to the Lord for and date it. I put my personal notes in what I call my "Gratitude Vase." Mine is a clear vase, or you could use a jar. It will help focus your mind back on Jesus and His daily provisions for your life. At the end of the year, or when I'm feeling a little down, I read the notes. I feel joy when I reflect on all God has done for me. Some of you may prefer to write down what you are grateful for in a personal journal. I also believe in intentionally showing gratitude by doing an act of kindness. It could be as simple as a smile to a stranger, sending a card of encouragement, buying someone you don't know a coffee or meal.

I also feel it is important to push beyond our "comfort level" of giving. It's easy to give in our "comfort level," but it's those times when we stretch beyond that, in turn, stretches our faith and increases our trust in the Lord.

Let's look at some other important attributes of a good steward.

A good steward operates with *integrity*. This requires being honest and doing what is right, regardless if anyone is looking or not. Our world culture will lead you to believe that occasionally a little compromise and untruth is okay. God knows it all and there is nothing we can hide from Him. If we desire God's blessings and favor, it is important we walk in integrity.

A good steward practices *self-control* and *discipline*. Similar to when you stop working out and your muscles shrink and become flabby again, so too are the "muscles" of self-control and discipline. You may not see those muscles if they are covered by fatty tissue from over indulgence (spending), but once you exercise them consistently, you will experience results: peace, contentment, even joy at having a balanced spending plan working for you each month. Bills will be paid on time, and you might even have a surplus at the end of the month.

Then, over time, you will start to not only *feel* the difference but *see* it also. That fat is now turning into muscle and you will be "out of the red" each month and "into the black." With steady progress, i.e., meditating daily on the scriptures provided that help shift your mindset from ownership to stewardship, prayer, following your spending plan, tracking your expenses, automating your savings, etc., you will start to see the definition in those muscles and the debt will fall away. Keep going and don't give up, no matter what! Even though you may have those days where you slip up and "miss a workout or two," remind yourself of where you're going and how it will feel once you reach that debt-free goal. It's worth every strain, every push, all the sweat and fatigue you will go through to spend less, save, invest more and reach that goal!

Study Questions:

What are the characteristics of good stewardship?

What areas are you already operating in good stewardship?

What areas in stewardship do you feel you need to improve?

What are some steps you will take to improve in these areas you have identified?

What are some ways you could show your gratitude consistently?

Are there some intentional acts of kindness you could incorporate into your life to bless others?

Prayer:

Father God, I desire to grow to be a good steward over my finances. Lord, I want to be the example of what it looks like to serve You with my whole heart. I want to be the best steward I can possibly be by using the resources You have entrusted to me in a way that glorifies You. Thank You, Father, for helping me to learn the characteristics of a good steward so that I can be financially free and be an even greater asset to Your Kingdom.

In Jesus' name. Amen.

Meditation:

"Honor the Lord with your wealth, with the first fruits of your crops; then your barns will be filled to overflowing, and your vats will brim over with new wine."

~ Proverbs 3: 9-10 NIV

"The generous will themselves be blessed, for they share their food with the poor."

~ Proverbs 22:9 NIV

"Do not eat the food of a begrudging host, do not crave his delicacies; for he is the person who is always thinking of the cost"

~ Proverbs 23:6-7 NIV

"Bring all the tithes into the storehouse, that there may be food in My house, And try Me now in this" Says the Lord of hosts, "If I will not open for you the windows of heaven And pour out for you such blessing That there will not be room enough to receive it"

~ Malachi 3:10 NKJV

"Give, and it will be given to you. A good measure, pressed down, shaken together and running over, will be poured into your lap. For with the measure you use, it will be measured to you."

~ Luke 6:38 NIV

Slave Mentality

"Let no debt remain outstanding except the debt to love one another, for the one who loves his fellowman has fulfilled the law."

~ Romans 13:7-8 NIV

Chapter 6

The Third Most Important Key to Wealth
"The Key to Wealth Is a Person's Ability to Use
Their Talents for the Greater Good of Others"
~ Darlene Cotton

The third most important key to wealth is to multiply your talents.

In this chapter I will share how to discover your talents and gifts, what it means for your future when you multiply your talents and what happens when you don't.

First, it is important you understand that my ultimate financial goal for you is not to track your spending to death, but instead adopt the abundant mindset and better stewardship characteristics, so you are not focused on *"Do I have enough?"* But instead focused on how can I be a better steward over the money I have been given and multiply it for the betterment of God's Kingdom.

As an example let's look at the scenario in *Matthew 25:14-29 NKJV*

"For the kingdom of heaven is like a man traveling to a far country, who called his own servants and delivered his goods to them. And to one he gave five talents, to another two, and to another one, to each according to his own ability; and immediately he went on a journey. Then he who had received the five talents went and traded with them, and made another five talents. And likewise he who had received two gained

more also. But he who had received one went and dug in the ground, and hid his lord's money. After a long time the lord of those servants came and settled their accounts with them. So he who had received five talents came and brought five other talents, saying 'Lord, you delivered to me five talents; look I have gained five more talents besides them.' His lord said to him, 'Well done, good and faithful servant; you were faithful over a few things, I will make you ruler over many things. Enter into the joy of the lord.' He also who had received two talents came and said, 'Lord, you delivered to me two talents; look, I have gained two more talents besides them.' His lord said to him, 'Well done, good and faithful servant; you have been faithful over a few things, I will make you ruler over many things. Enter into the joy of your lord.' Then he who had received one talent came and said, 'Lord, I knew you to be a hard man, reaping where you have not sown, and gathering where you have not scattered seed. And I was afraid, and went and hid your talent in the ground. Look, there you have what is yours.' But the lord answered and said to him, 'You wicked and lazy servant, you knew that I reap where I have not sown, and gather where I have not scattered seed. So you ought to have deposited my money with the bankers, and at my coming I would have received back my interest. Therefore take the talent from him, and give it to him who has ten talents. For to everyone who has, more will be given, and he will have abundance; but from him who does not have, even what he has will be taken away."

~ Matthew 25:14-29 NKJV

The talents represent the resources God has entrusted to each one of us, such as money, gifts, talents, and time.

The gifts I am referring to are those God-given, supernatural gifts such as the gift of prophecy, healing, teaching, intercession/prayer and discernment. A talent is a specific skill set that comes naturally and/or self-developed over time such as, singing, painting or athletic skill

If you have not discovered your talents and gifts here are a few questions to ask yourself:

➤ What brings you fulfillment and joy when doing it?

➤ What is it that you do that contributes value to others with little to no effort? In other words, it seems to come naturally.

➤ What are some of your favorite topics to discuss?

➤ What is your favorite section in the bookstore or library?

➤ If money were not an issue, what would you do as a profession?

➤ What cause are you passionate about and would love to be involved with, but may have felt like you didn't have enough time or money?

Once you have discovered your gifts and talents, the next question to ask yourself is, "How can I invest those gifts, talents, and money in a way that will not only impact those closest to me, but also reach people beyond my immediate inner-circle for the glory of the Lord?"

I encourage you to start first with being a good steward over the people and things closest to you.

This means, those you interact with on a daily basis, which would consist of yourself, spouse, children, friends, finances, job, co-workers, business and employees.

"His lord said to him, 'Well done, good and faithful servant; you were faithful over a few things, I will make you ruler over many things. Enter into the joy of your lord.'"

~ Matthew 25:21 NKJV

As you consistently seek to make deposits of your talents into others for His Kingdom, just like you gain interest over time as you deposit money into the bank, God will bring the increase into your life. He will line up the resources and bring the people. He just needs your trust and obedience in order to guide you on the path.

Pastor T.D. Jakes once said, *"Money should not be the mission; Money should help fund our mission."*

Ask yourself, "How can I add value to others by doing something I love?"

I strongly believe it is important to discover your gifts and talents and follow your passion and your purpose and not the money. When you follow purpose *first,* the money will come…

"…Seek first the kingdom of God and His righteousness and all these things shall be added on to you."

~ Matthew 6:33 NKJV

Find something you love to do and master it, so you can be the best for you and others.

If you are doing what you would do, whether you got paid or not, because it is fulfilling, then you are on the right track. I recommend to continue developing that skill set by learning more through classes, finding a mentor, reading books, etc. Work hard so you can become an expert in that field and impact even more people for the Lord.

Don't fall into the trap like the servant who had the one talent and was so afraid to lose what he was given, holding on tight to the little he had. As a result there was no outlet for increase. The moment he buried his one talent, he cut off the flow to obtaining more. Just like your talents and gifts need to be shared, your money also needs to circulate. This includes investing our money in a way that brings increase to the body of Christ.

It's important as followers of Christ that we recognize that all good and perfect gifts come from the Lord. It all belongs to Him. He expects us to not only keep from wastefully spending, but also to take the money and, through His wisdom, multiply and grow our finances to contribute to the advancement of His kingdom.

Wealth is for all believers to receive; not as the world giveth, but by the grace of our Lord and Savior.

Satan knows that wealth is ours as believers of Jesus because he had the opportunity to receive his blessings. However, he let pride and greed take precedence, which led to rebuke and God casting him from Heaven. The devil missed his opportunity. Do not allow him to trick you into missing yours.

This is what the Lord, your Redeemer, the Holy One of Israel says, *"I am the Lord your God, who teaches you to profit (benefit) Who leads you in the way that you should go. Oh, that you had paid attention to My commandments! Then your peace and prosperity would have been like a (flowing) river, And your righteousness (the holiness and purity of the nation) like the (abundant) waves of the sea."*

~ Isaiah 48:17-18 AMP

The Holy Spirit is our guide, our protection from being misled. The Holy Spirit teaches us to profit. Not only will you profit, but you will profit with peace. I am not saying it will come without challenges and tribulations. What I am saying is that when those challenges come as you are walking in the will of God, you will be able to rest in His peace and not be moved by your circumstances.

Here are some tips to help position yourself to receive the wealth God has for you.

➤ Follow the Holy Spirit and it will lead and teach you to profit
➤ Ask God for wisdom to make wise decisions
➤ Practice the characteristics of good stewardship
➤ Maximize your time

Maximize Your Time

According to a November 2015 article in Nielsen Report, the average American watches nearly 35 hours of TV a week (live and DVR). It went on to state the average American adult aged 35-49 watches so much TV, it is almost a full time job. A Huffington Post article published November 2,

2015, said research conducted by a British psychologist shows that young adults use their smartphones on average of 5 hours a day. That's roughly one-third of their waking hours!

As you learned in the earlier chapters, in order to accomplish living a life free of financial and spiritual bondage, you will need to change your current thinking. And focus less on being a consumer and more on being an investor and/or innovator.

> *Take the time you would typically use to watch TV and invest in yourself.*

Where will you be in life a year or two from now, if you cut the average time spent on smartphones and TV in half, and instead spent that time investing in yourself, discovering and developing your gifts and finding ways to create a profit doing it? This will allow you an opportunity to increase your cash flow to pay off your debt and live the life you truly desire.

We're not put on the earth to live a mediocre life.

God loves us too much to allow us to live the mundane life having no challenges and difficulties.

I have learned it's through my difficult moments that I experience the most personal growth, because

I am forced to exercise the most patience and develop the most creativity.

The Bible says we were created in His image, so the truth is, we all are created for greatness!

The solution is found in seeking God daily in His word, spending time in worship, and praising Him. It also is important to ask Him for wisdom and guidance, then listening, receiving, trusting, and being obedient to what He tells you to do. That includes heeding the warnings of the Holy Spirit to keep your eyes fixed on Jesus and to realize it is His works in and through you to do His good and perfect will.

Beware of those who consciously, or subconsciously, put you on a pedestal, and idolize the gift inside you, instead of the giver and creator in you. If you internalize and entertain this misdirected praise, over time pride will take root. It will try to choke out the harvest God is setting up for you and others to reap on His behalf. So, stand firm, stay focused and let nothing move you as you work in excellence unto the Lord.

Study Questions:

What are three ways in which you could develop or enhance your gifts and talents?

What resources might you need to accomplish it?

What are some creative ways you can invest your money, gifts, and talents to increase God's Kingdom?

The ultimate reason God has gifted each of us with unique talents is for sharing God's love and gospel with people. Let it be our mission as believers to point others to the good news of His gospel.

Prayer:

Father, God I thank you for the love you have for me and for your peace that surpasses all understanding. Lord, help me to know and walk confidently in my true identity as a joint heir with Jesus. Give me boldness to seek out, discover and develop my gifts/talents for your kingdom. And help me to walk in obedience, following your path for my life and receiving the prosperity that only You can give.

In Jesus name. Amen.

Meditation:

"Do not be conformed to this world (this cage), (fashioned after and adapted to its external, superficial customs), but transformed (changed) by the (entire) renewal of your mind (by its new ideals and its new attitude), so that you may prove (for yourselves) what is the good and acceptable and perfect will of God, even the thing which is good and acceptable and perfect (in His sight for you.) For by the grace (unmerited favor of God) given to me I warn everyone among you not to estimate and think of himself more highly than he ought (not to have an exaggerated opinion of his own importance), but to rate his ability with sober judgment, each according to the degree of faith apportioned by God to him."

~ Romans 12:2-3 AMP

"...thanks be to God! He gives us the victory through our Lord Jesus Christ. Therefore, dear brothers and sisters, stand firm. Always give fully to the work of the Lord, because you know that your labor is not in vain."

~ I Corinthians 15:57-58 NIV

"Give no sleep to your eyes, Nor slumber to your eyelids. Deliver yourself like a gazelle from the hunter, And like a bird from the hand of the fowler."

~ Proverbs 6:4-5 NKJV

"Thus says the Lord, your Redeemer, and The Holy One of Israel: 'I am the Lord your God who teaches you to profit, who leads you by the way you should go.'"

~ Isaiah 48:17 NKJV

"The thief does not come except to steal, and to kill, and to destroy. I have come that they may have life, and that they may have it more abundantly."

~ John 10:10 NKJV

Chapter 7

VISION The Power of Imagination
"Where there is no vision, the people perish."
~ Proverbs 29:18 KJV

Vision is a thought or concept formed by the power of imagination. Our imagination is a gift from God. It allows us to obtain a visual of our dreams and aspirations before they happen. I believe imagination helps catapult you forward to being and doing all the amazing things God has equipped each one of us to accomplish.

According to Webster's dictionary, vision is "the ability to think about or plan the future with imagination or wisdom."

I think most would agree it takes both wisdom and imagination to form a clear and concise vision. Imagination paints the picture to your vision. It creates the emotion behind moving forward in your vision for your future. It is a part of the transformation of going from where you are currently in life to where you desire to go. It starts in our mind with thoughts, words, and ultimately our actions.

"For as he thinks in his heart, so is he…"
~ Proverbs 23:7 NKJV

An important step to obtaining the desire God has put in your heart is believing God's word in Mark 10:27 NIV *"...through God ALL things are possible"* for yourself. How many times in life do we speak those words for our friends, family, or neighbor, but never truly believe in God to do it for us? God loves you beyond what you could ever imagine. I dare you to meditate on His word and believe in Him to bring those desires in your heart to pass in your life.

I want you to take some time and dream...

What are those things you desire for your life?

Remember to allow yourselves to dream big, and expand your imagination, because it is not in *our* strength, but the Lord's that these things will manifest. We serve a big God of unlimited power!

Visualize how you would like your life to be. Ask yourself the following questions...

➢ What does your ideal relationship with your spouse, fiancé, children, siblings, parents and friends look like?

➢ What changes do you see happening with your health and fitness?

➢ What types of foods will you eat to become healthier? What will your body look like because of eating healthier and exercising more? How will you feel in this new body?

➢ What will you do for fun? Who will enjoy those fun times with you? What vacations will you take? Where will you travel?

➤ What are your financial goals? Do you have a certain net worth you want to obtain? How much monthly cash flow do you see yourself making? And what will you do with it?

➤ If your goal is to become debt-free, what will that freedom look like for you?

➤ One thing being debt-free will give you is more options of how to spend your time, so think about how you will spend it.

➤ What impact do you want to make in your community, city, state, country, or world? Who will you be impacting? A certain social or economic group? Adults, children, or both? What age groups? What impact will you strive to make in their lives?

➤ Will you be running your own business or will you be making a powerful impact as part of someone else's business or organization?

➤ In what areas of your personal (household) and business will you employ help with daily activities, so that you can focus your efforts on the twenty percent that creates the greatest difference in your life?

In the space below. List dreams you have and the changes you want to make to get there.

_____

_____

_____

_____

_____

_____

_____

_____

_____

_____

_____

_____

_____

_____

_____

_____

_____

_____

_____

_____

_____

_____

_____

_____

_____

_____

Slave Mentality

Creating a Vision Board:

A vision board is an illustration of the things to come, if we don't give up! There is something about picturing it before it happens along with writing it down that helps make it a reality.

There is no right or wrong way to create your vision board. This exercise is where you give yourself the freedom to envision your dreams. You can make one board with your personal and business/ministry goals, using a collage of pictures that represent your vision for your life. Include photos of yourself, family, others with whom you want to partner, and affirmations/words that reflect your thoughts, ambitions and desires. Words that speak to your spirit. DREAM BIG.

I recommend two separate vision boards. One for personal and another for the vision of your business/career and ministry work.

Also, try not to place too many items close together, to avoid cluttering your board, which will represent chaos versus clarity and harmony.

Take time daily to look at your vision board and internalize those things you have envisioned and placed on your board as they begin to manifest. Don't waste your time entertaining those limiting beliefs that are trying to get in your way. Instead, shift your thoughts to believing the life you envisioned can be yours.

What I mean by this is that we must be intentional in the thoughts we allow to occupy our minds. Do not allow doubt (unbelief) to cloud your mind. You must feed yourself positivity. Read God's word. Write down scriptures that "speak" to your spirit, mediate on those words and show gratitude daily.

Every day be intentional to take action that brings you closer to your dream becoming your new reality.

I remember when I was twenty-one and went to Sacramento, California, for a family reunion. At that time I lived in Anchorage, Alaska, where I'd been born. I'd never lived anywhere else except San Diego when I was very young. Being in California for the reunion opened my eyes to a different way of life. For one, the weather was drastically different. Sacramento is sunny and warm most of the time, compared to the long winters in Alaska. There are a variety of concerts, amusement parks, and shopping malls—as well as being able to get on the freeway to drive to another city or state in the U.S., whereas in Alaska you must travel through Canada to get to the rest of the U.S.

I looked at all the major companies in Sacramento and saw a multitude of opportunities. I felt California had a lot to offer and wanted to experience more of life, so I returned to Alaska and put a plan together to move to California. I cut back on my spending by drastically limiting my entertainment activities and eating out…started paying off my credit card debt, saving money, and researching jobs in Sacramento. I'd accumulated enough vacation time at my job to take three weeks off. I put together a résumé and compiled a list of jobs where I could apply.

While I waited with hope and expectation, I envisioned myself living there—the activities I would be doing, where I might work and which part of the city I would live in.

When I went to California the next time, I was on a mission and had a plan. I had lined up multiple job interviews. While I was there, a friend was talking to a customer at her job. This person worked for the courthouse. My friend asked her if there were positions open. (At that time I was working for the courts in Alaska.) There was a position open, so I applied, interviewed, and got the job!

My point in sharing this story is in the hope you too will allow yourself to dream. And pursue your dream by putting a plan in place and taking steps toward making your dream a reality. Although you will at times grow weary when it seems like it is taking forever, don't give up! As your desires and dreams align with His will for your life, it will come to pass!

Although this opportunity and move was a blessing, it did not come without its challenges. I had to start the job in two weeks! The first person I called after getting the news was my mom. However, I didn't get the response I'd expected. Though she'd been supportive when I started the process, she was upset that I was moving away.

That was difficult for me because I value my mom's opinion and support. Her approval was important to me. I was torn emotionally because my plan had come together but my mom wasn't happy. She called friends and relatives to ask them to talk me out of the move. Soon that excitement turned into resentment toward her.

Yet, I had to follow my dream. If I didn't, I would have asked myself *"What if?"* for the rest of my life. I figured, if I *did* go but failed, I could only blame myself. But if I didn't go, I would always blame her.

My decision to accept the opportunity was life changing, and one that brought so much happiness!

I was able to experience things in life I would not have if I had stayed in Alaska. God had already mapped out my destiny. I met some great people with whom I developed very close friendships with and have become a part of my family. God also used me to impact other people's lives. While living there, I joined an organization called "Big Brothers, Big Sisters" and mentored a young girl for a few years. We developed a close relationship. She was my bridesmaid when I got married years later. I also had the privilege of serving as a volunteer chaplain in the Juvenile Detention Center teaching Bible study to the teens incarcerated at that time. Through that opportunity, I was blessed to develop trust and build friendships with the teens there. One young lady in particular, with whom I developed a special bond and consider "my little sister," remains in contact to this day. Not to mention Sacramento was the place I met my loving husband while attending a church where I was nurtured and grew in my relationship with the Lord.

My mother and I got over our differences and have a great relationship now. She has been one of my biggest supporters.

So, let me ask you...what is that "thing" or "relationship" where you believe God is telling you to take a chance?

Don't live your life in the *"what if"* stage. I haven't always followed through on things I had a desire to do and, to this day, I sometimes wonder "what if" on a few things I quit.

We want *fewer "what if's"* in our lives and *more "I gave it all I had"* because, when we give something or someone all we have and leave the results to our all-knowing God, we can't go wrong.

Study Questions:

I want you to take a moment and write down three things you have a desire to do but have been putting off out of fear, doubt, lack of resources, lack of confidence, etc.

1)

2)

3)

Below are some steps I would like you to follow:

➤ Seek God - it will take consistent seeking and willingness to listen. Many times when we pray, we ask God for something, but we don't take the time to listen to Him for the answer.

"...thus says the Lord, who created you, O Jacob, And He who formed you, O Israel:" Fear not, I have redeemed you; I have called you by your name; And when you pass through the waters, I will be with you; And through the rivers, they shall not overflow you. When you walk through the fire, you shall not be burned, Nor shall the flame scorch you. For I am the Lord your God, The Holy One of Israel, your Savior..."

~ Isaiah 43: 1-3 NKJV

As you continue to seek Him, God will guide you and bring resources to help you.

➢ Recognize it is not merely about you and your family, it is about His greater purpose and plan for all the other people who need what He has given you to do.

It will require your faith to trust and obey God's instructions.

God wants to do a miracle in your life so you can be a witness to His power and testify that He is real. He is our Savior and the one and only living God, still working miracles in the lives of those who believe in Him.

We must always keep in our heart and mind that it is the Holy Spirit/Jesus who lives inside each believer. It is the Holy Spirit who gives us power to do great things in Jesus' name. Our focus cannot start off or become about us building a name for ourselves. For if it does, we will lose focus and fellowship with the Lord and could destroy the great dream and purpose that God placed on the inside of each of us.

This life you have envisioned can be yours, but it will require you to get out of your own way. What I mean by this is you have to be intentional in the thoughts you allow to occupy your mind.

➢ Seek out godly people who share the values and have obtained the accomplishments you wish to have. Attend workshops, watch online videos of those individuals who are where you want to be and can teach you how to get there. Invest in a personal or business mentor or coach to help you get from where you are to where you want to be.

An important lesson I learned when working with a coach is simply to apply the principles taught immediately. When we put off taking action, we allow other things to take priority. You must be committed to the vision, and having an accountability partner helps. However you have to do the work!

Someone once said, *"No one can do the push-ups for you."* Meaning don't expect results if you are not consistently putting in the work. At the same time, do not beat yourself up when you have a setback. Allow yourself some grace. Start again. Tomorrow is a new day!

Prayer:
Father God, I seek you and ask that you align my thoughts and imagination with the great plans

You have for my life, that I may see, believe, and receive the great vision, knowing that all things are possible with you, Lord. I believe that if You have given me this purpose and plan for my future, You have equipped me with all I need to obtain it. I trust You, Lord, with my whole heart. Please direct my path and lead me to fulfill all You have put inside of me for the betterment of others and myself. I love You, Lord.

In Jesus' name. Amen.

Meditation:

"For I know the plans and thoughts that I have for you," says the Lord. *"Plans for peace and well-being and not for disaster to give you a future and a hope."*

~ Jeremiah 29:11 AMP

"He sought God in the days of Zechariah, who had an understanding in the visions of God; and as long as he sought the Lord, God made him prosper."

~ 2 Chronicles 26:5 NKJV

"My people are destroyed by their lack of knowledge…"

~ Hosea 4:6 NKJV

"The utterance of him who hears the words of God, and the knowledge of the Most High, who sees the vision of the Almighty…"

~ Numbers 24:16 NKJV

"Write the vision and make it plain on tablets, that he may run who reads it. For the vision is yet for an appointed time, but at the end, it will speak and it will not lie. Though it tarries, wait for it because it will surely come; it will not tarry."

~ Habakkuk 2:2-3 NKJV

The Greatest Asset to Invest in is You!

"I will praise You, for I am fearfully and wonderfully made; Marvelous are Your works, And that my soul knows very well"
`~Psalm 139:14

The greatest asset you have other than your relationship with your creator is *you*, His fearfully and wonderfully made creation. God loves you and has made you unique with a specific purpose. He has placed special gifts and talents within and it is up to you to discover and develop them.

Now that you have taken the time to read and apply the principles in this book, you should have a good idea of your purpose. Some of you may have known your purpose before reading the book, but never taking the next steps of developing and walking in it.

You learned the importance of focusing on positive, uplifting thoughts, i.e. biblical scriptures. You applied tools to shift your focus from one of lack into the abundance God has already provided. You learned that money is a good servant but a terrible master, and the importance of taking control of your finances. You learned that getting extraordinary results requires a radical change. You were provided with creative ideas to think "outside the box" to earn additional income and get out of debt quicker. You learned the three important keys to wealth: wisdom, good stewardship and multiplying your talents.

However, all this great information is not enough to create a lasting change in your financial and spiritual life. It will take consistent repetition of self-discipline, dedication, guidance, and accountability to eventually make it a lifelong habit and lifestyle. This accountability can come from a spouse, close relative, or friend only if that person is already living out these principles regularly in their own life.

The simplest and fastest way to get there is through a mentor, one-on-one coaching, or group coaching program. You notice I said simplest and fastest, but not easiest. Any time you are making a drastic change, it comes with irritation, frustration, hurt, anger, struggles, and stumbles. This is why it helps to have a coach, mentor, or accountability partner. Someone who understands what you are going through because they have been through similar situations and experienced true transformation in their own life.

Mentality Shift offers that support, encouragement, guidance, and accountability through a variety of coaching, tools, and resources. Our programs, courses and complimentary discover session can be found at www.mentalityshift.net

Are You Prepared for the Battle Ahead?

"For though we walk in the flesh, we do not war according to the flesh. For the weapons of our warfare are not carnal but mighty in God for pulling down strongholds"
~ II Corinthians 10:3-4 NKJV

I would be setting you up for failure if I did not mention spiritual warfare and the part it plays in our lives. Spiritual warfare is real. Please do not be tricked into believing that if you do all that is in this book, you will *"ride into the sunset,"* living the life of prosperity. The enemy is real. According to the scripture found in John 10:10, it says, *"The enemy comes only to kill, steal and destroy..."* He will come after you to derail you. However, remember he has already been defeated by our Father. The devil is like a dog on a leash with a big bark. Our Father has control over the devil and his schemes to kill, steal, and destroy our lives. All that have received Jesus as their Lord and Savior belong to the Father and are under His authority, protection, and care. However we must equip ourselves through His word and put on the *"whole armor."*

...be strong in the Lord (draw your strength from Him and be empowered through your union with Him) and in the power of His (boundless) might. Put on the full armor of God (for His precepts are like the splendid armor of a heavily armed solider), so that you may be able to (successfully) stand up against all the schemes and the strategies and the deceits of the devil. For our struggle is not against flesh and blood

99

(contending only with the physical opponents), but against the rulers, against the powers, against the world forces of this (present) darkness, against spiritual forces of wickedness in the heavenly (supernatural) places. Therefore, put on the complete armor of God, so that you will be able to (successfully) resist and stand your ground in the evil (of danger), and having done everything (that the crisis demands), to stand firm (in your place, fully prepared, immovable, victorious). So stand firm and hold your ground, having tightened the wide band of truth (personal integrity, moral courage) around your waist and having put on the breastplate of righteousness (an upright heart), and having strapped on your feet the gospel of peace in preparation (to face the enemy with firm-footed stability and the readiness produced by the good news). Above all, lift up the (protective) shield of faith with which you can extinguish all the flaming arrows of the evil one. And take the helmet of salvation, and the sword of the Spirit, which is the Word of God. With all prayer and petition pray (with specific requests) at all times (on every occasion and in every season) in the Spirit, and with this in view, stay alert with all perseverance and petition (interceding in prayer) for all God's people."

~ Ephesians 6:11-18 AMP

I recommend reading *The Three Battlegrounds* by Francis Frangipane in regards to overcoming spiritual attack.

Do You Have a Relationship with Jesus?

Jesus loves you and desires nothing more than to have a personal relationship with you.

If you have not received Jesus as your Lord and Savior, I would like to give you an opportunity to invite Jesus into your heart and receive salvation through Him. If you are ready to make a decision to accept Him as your Lord and Savior begin by saying this prayer out loud...

Prayer:

Father God, I come to you in the name of Jesus, you said *"... whoever calls on the name of the Lord Shall be saved"* -Acts 2:21 NKJV. I am calling on you now! Your Word also says *"If you confess with your mouth the Lord Jesus and believe in your heart that God has raised Him from the dead, you will be saved. For with the heart one believes unto righteousness, and with the mouth confession is made unto salvation."* - Romans 10:9-10 NKJV

I confess that I have sinned. I repent and ask for your forgiveness. I confess that Jesus is Lord. I believe in my heart that God the Father raised Him from the dead. I ask you to come into my heart, cleanse me of my sins and become my Lord and Savior. I am now born again...and have eternal salvation through Jesus Christ.

Congratulations on your new beginning in a life with Christ!

"Therefore, if anyone is in Christ, he is a new creation; old things have passed away; behold all things have become new"

~ 2 Corinthians 5:17 NKJV

I encourage you to spend time with God everyday praying and reading the Bible and seeking fellowship with other believers consistently.

Conclusion

Financial and spiritual freedom in Kingdom living is when you trust in God completely to provide for you and your family in every area of your life including your finances. You know who you are and whose you are. You are Kingdom-minded and being a good steward over all God has entrusted to you by operating in love, peace, servanthood, self-control, and investing and multiplying those resources by walking in your God-given purpose.

My hope is that you focus on becoming debt-free so you are no longer a slave to the things of the world. Money is *one* source God has blessed us with to bless others and show His love. We cannot afford to operate in a fear-based mindset while, at the same time, strive for financial and spiritual freedom. It's only by our faith in God, being led by the Holy Spirit and loving God's people that we will be able to make the greatest impact in this world...and experience the abundant life God has given us the opportunity to receive.

Bibliography

All Scripture quotations, unless otherwise indicated, are the New King James Version®. Copyright © 1982 by Thomas Nelson. Used by permission. All rights reserved.

All Scripture quotation marked NIV are taken from THE HOLY BIBLE, NEW INTERNATIONAL VERSION®, NIV® Copyright © 1973, 1978, 1984, 2011 by Biblica, Inc.® Used by permission. All rights reserved worldwide.

All Scripture quotation marked AMP are taken from The Amplified Bible Copyright © 2015 by The Lockman Foundation, La Habra, CA 90631. All rights reserved. For Permission To Quote information visit http://www.lockman.org/

The "Amplified" trademark is registered in the United States Patent and Trademark Office by The Lockman Foundation. Use of this trademark requires the permission of The Lockman Foundation.

Introduction: My Journey to a Life of Milk and Honey
Redemption & Advancement- www.redeem-advance.org

Chapter 2- TAKE Control of Your Financial Life
www.michigancounselingassociation.com/uploa
ds/2/6/3/4/2634297_financial_education.pdf

Chapter 3- Shift Your Debt Elimination Efforts into Overdrive
Debt Statistics found at U.S. Census Bureau and
Federal Reserve
www.studentaid.edu.gov last accessed 8/8/18
www.Wikipedia.com definition of Joint Venture
last accessed 8/9/1

Chapter 5- The Second Most Important Key to Wealth
As author Randy Alcorn stated in his book "The
Treasure Principle", *"Whenever we think we are owners,*
it's a red flag. We should be thinking like stewards,
investment managers, always looking for the best place to
invest the Owner's money.